Babys for Seals

by Kathy Furgang

Many harbor seals live on the Pacific coast.

Why Do Seals Need Help?

Harbor seals live in many oceans around the world. They stay close to land. They spend half their lives in water. They spend the other half on land, resting.

Seal pups cannot find food for themselves.

The seals also come onto land to have babies, called pups. The mother seals must look for food for their pups. They leave their pups on shore until they return with food.

Seal pups wait for their mothers.

Seal pups face dangers on shore. Seals have flippers instead of feet. They cannot run away from animals that want to catch them. Bears, eagles, and dogs are a danger to the pups. Humans can be a danger, too!

The seals come to shore onto busy beaches.

How Do People Help?

The seal pups also get help from humans. On some beaches, people watch the pups. They are babysitters for the seal pups! They guard the seal pups day and night.

People must guard the pups from a distance. If they get too close, the pups will become afraid. The mother seals may also be afraid to return to their pups.

6

Pupping season lasts through the summer.

The seal sitters make sure that people stay away from the baby seals. They watch that dogs and other animals do not bother the pups.

The pups rest until their mothers come back. Then they may return to the water. But they may be back again to rest on the shore.